OVERCOMING A LIFE OF TURMOIL
LOSING A CHILD IN THE MIDST OF IT

BARBARA JOHNSON SIMPSON

Overcoming A Life of Turmoil

Copyright © 2016 Barbara J Simpson Author, LLC

All rights reserved.

ISBN-10: 0692858067

ISBN-13: 9780692858066

No part of this book may be reproduced or transmitted in any form or by any means, electronic or mechanical, including photocopying, recording, or by any information storage and retrieval system, without permission in writing from the copyright owner.

Scripture quotations marked KJV are from the Holy Bible,
King James Version (Authorized Version). First published in 1611. Quoted from the KJV Classic Reference Bible, Copyright © 1983 by The Zondervan Corporation. Other scripture references are New King James Bible Version (NKJV) Amplified Bible Version (AMP) American Standard Version (ASV) New International Version (NIV) English Standard Version (ESV).

Any people depicted in images and such images are being used for illustrative purposes only. There were certain names omitted to protect the rights and confidentiality of others. There were certain parts of the story left out or omitted and partially written to protect the rights and confidentiality of others. Print information available on the last page.

DEDICATION

Looking up, I would like to dedicate this book to my princess my daughter.
"Brit Britt"

This I know my sweet dearest "Brit Britt" that the divine is not something high above us. Its heaven, it is in the earth, it is inside of us. When I cry, I cry tears of joy for I know that one day we will be together again. Departed but redeemed, you will forever be in my heart.

I love you my sweet Princess
Brittnay Nashay

Overcoming A Life of Turmoil

CONTENTS

Acknowledgments

Forward

Message of Hope And Encouragement (BJS)

1	An Unexpected Tragedy	8
2	Turmoil And Confusion	17
3	Dealing With What Was Before Me	25
4	Living For My Purpose, So I Thought	31
5	I Shall Not Die! But Live!	46
6	God Revealed To Me Who I was In Him	51

Praise Break	61
As I Look Back And Think Things Over	62
The Confession	64
Christian Bed Time Prayer (RIH)	65
Conclusion	66
Final Thoughts	67
About The Author	70

Barbara Johnson Simpson

ACKNOWLEDGMENTS

First, I would like to thank my Heavenly Father for giving me the strength, the endurance and leading me through this process. I owe such a great big thanks to the people who helped and supported me during the writing of this book.

A special thanks and honor to my mother Dorothy Johnson.

I would like to thank my father the late Charlie Johnson, Sr.

I also want to give great homage to Pastor Prophetess Helen Godfrey-Smith of the Greater Provision Christian Church Shreveport, Louisiana for your caring for me as I engaged in spiritual warfare. I know it was not an easy task counseling me one on one through this journey. However, **Proverbs 24:6 says, for by wise guidance, you will wage war, and in abundance of counselors, there is victory.**

I would like to thank Dr. Nathaniel Manning in his mentoring, advisement and inspiration.

Lastly, I would like to thank Kim Clayton for inspiring while I was preparing to write my book. She encouraged and kept me lifted up in prayer as I began to write what God the Father placed on the inside of me.

Overcoming A Life of Turmoil

To My Beloved Sons I Love You!

FORWARD

We are all given a blank canvas to paint a portrait of our interpretation of life. The types of brushes we use often influence the strokes of our journey as well as how the colors of our life will blend. This book illuminates the author's canvas that has not always been placed on an easel; has not always been placed under the proper lighting and most definitely has not embraced subject matters that lend the inspiration needed to complete the portrait.

Avid readers will discover the maturity of this writer and her ability to help the reader acquire a taste for a genre of work based on an author's ability to connect with and convict their hearts. This book replicates the story of many women from various walks of life, ethnic groups, faiths, and socio-economic statuses. The book is the voice of the woman within; the silent woman; the broken and abused woman who finds a way to mask her pain by fashionably dressing her outward appearance. It is the story of someone with a façade of success who has intimately interwoven the threads of failure into her daily existence. It characterizes a woman from a middle class family in the small Bible-belt city of Shreveport, Louisiana who lives in a city filled with individuals who have become actors. She too has become an actor, so consumed with her role, and rehearsed lines, until she loses reality. Each person she encounters throughout her life has taken a piece of her. They have taken a piece of her mind, her heart, her spirit, and her soul. They have left her feeling empty almost void of life. They have built platforms and stages from her script, never crediting her work. She finds herself learning how to become numb to the pain of the wounds, which were, filled with salt sprinkled from the hands she considered friends and sometimes her own family. The author speaks of her happy times, her accomplishments, her dreams, and her vision. The reader begins to see the author's life through 3-D lens, getting to know the real Barbara Johnson-Simpson up close and personal. Ironically, as you learn who the author is, you begin to learn who you are, the real authentic you.

I have known this writer for over ten years, both professionally and personally. However, I only knew her on the surface. In this book, she allows the layers of her life to be peeled back and her vulnerability exposed. She speaks and shares lessons that were not taught or learned in the chambers of higher education, but instead lessons learned through the University of Life. There are lessons on purpose, manipulation, infidelity, intimacy, and relationships. There are also lessons of redemption, love, forgiveness, and transformation. This holistic book will provide hope and healing. It is a book of broken pieces mended together by the artistry of our Creator through true repentance.

By: Kim Clayton

Overcoming A Life of Turmoil

Author
Barbara Johnson Simpson

Barbara Johnson Simpson

We are hard pressed on every side, but not crushed; perplexed, but not in despair; persecuted, but not abandoned; struck down, but not destroyed.
2 Corinthians 4:8-9

MESSAGE OF HOPE AND ENCOURAGEMENT

By: Author Barbara Johnson Simpson (BJS)

Life is about choices. How often do we make those choices out of emotions and feelings? In the King James Version of **Proverbs Chapter 3:5-6 it says to trust in the Lord with all thine heart; and lean not unto thine own understanding, In all thy ways acknowledge Him, and he shall direct thy paths.**

Allow God to be your compass and provide the direction that he knows is the best and beneficial for your individual needs. When making choices and decisions we must rely on God and know that he will direct our path. God is so faithful and trustworthy, we must trust that he knows what He's doing.

With God's transformation of my life I have written this book to help encourage you in our Heavenly Father, because through it all I've learned to let the Lord be my spiritual compass as well as the importance of **Proverbs 16:3 which tells us to entrust your work to the LORD and your planning will succeed.**

CHAPTER 1

AN UNEXPECTED TRAGEDY

I lost my home and there I was homeless. My life at that time had little to no direction at all. Could you imagine me starting a new job as the director of a homeless shelter for women and children? I was involved in two relationships, while at the same time feeling confused about which one of my guy friends I was going to choose. You see, in the beginning, I was living with and going back and forth between both of them without them knowing it. I finally left one altogether and began staying with the other.

After I made my choice, I completely moved in, and he quickly purchased marriage license for us to get married. However, I did not go through with it. He was very hurt by my response and it caused an argument between us. It was so intense that I left the house and did not know where I was going. However, I ended up going to the duck pond. While I was sitting there, I began starring at the water crying. I was very emotionally confused and didn't know how to handle it so I called my other guy friend because I wanted him to reassure me of the love he had for me. Meanwhile, as I was talking to him, my phone rang; it was the other guy calling; the one who asked me to marry him. I answered and I told him that I was at the duck pond. I went there because I was under a lot of pressure about what took place between us back at the house. I needed a peace of mind and I didn't know where else to turn.

While I was crying, everything seem to hit me at once so I cried even more about losing my home, and starting a new job as a director at the homeless shelter. In the midst of me crying, he comes to the pond and ask me to come back home with him. I replied, please give me some time to think things over because at this point I didn't know whether or not I wanted to get a hotel room or return to his house. He decided to leave me alone, I began to cry again, and as I cried, I heard the voice of the Lord say Pray for Brittnay. Immediately, I prayed. In my mind I, thought God was telling me to pray based off the disagreeing conversation that my daughter and I had earlier that day; pertaining to her moving into her own apartment. This was the second time we had a disagreement because she desired to have her friend move in with her, after I told her I was totally against that. Needless to say, I prayed this prayer; Father, God; whatever your will is for Brittany's life, let it be done. Thinking back as I prayed that prayer I cried so hard and at the time I didn't know why. One thing for sure, I would not have prayed that prayer, if I knew my daughter's life would have been in jeopardy. I would have prayed for healing from her juvenile diabetes.

After gathering myself together, I decided to return to my guy friend's house. Upon, returning I turned my cell phone completely off and I told him I did not want to be bothered because I was going to bed for the night. Approximately, thirty minutes later, there was a pounding on the door, as I looked out the window; I saw several of my family members. I began to ponder what could have happened. Immediately, I knew something was wrong. Nevertheless, they all gathered in the room to tell me what was going on, and I began screaming asking them not to tell me anything; because I knew, and had a feeling deep within that it had to be death.

Moreover, they told me the painful news that my daughter had passed away. Sure enough, what I felt was right. At first, I wouldn't let them tell me what happen because I did not know how I was going to react. I was in a state of shock! I wanted to believe that it was someone else in the family instead of my Brittnay. After all, my daughter was not sick! Her only illness was that she suffered from juvenile diabetes.

After receiving the news, we all traveled to my mother's house to try to make sense of all this. As I continued to cry, I desire to know what really happened to my daughter so I spoke with the deputy corner and they said that she died in her sleep by natural causes.

As time went on, my family and I sat down to discuss the funeral arrangements. After having time to reflect, I didn't realize the reality of what I was facing with burying my daughter without life insurance; this instantly sent me into panic mode! I couldn't sleep at all that night. However, God had already set things in order. He was working things out and I didn't even know it.

The next morning more family came by to offer their support. A close friend of the family came over as well, to pray with me. This close friend assigned to me three of my own personal keepers who were so gracious to me throughout the whole process. This friend also gave me the money to pay for the funeral. Can you believe, that in the midst of all the turmoil in my life, God was still good! As I mention earlier God had already set things in order. This reminds me of what the scripture says in **Philippians 4:19, but my God will supply all your need according to his riches in glory by Christ Jesus.**

Now it's time for the funeral arrangements to be put into action. I had to make some very hard decisions. I decided that there was not going to be a family hour. My belief is that the funeral serves enough purpose, no need to have two services. Therefore, I had a beautiful home going service for my precious beautiful daughter.

Brittnay died September 2, 2013. Reality began to set in, and I realized that I would never see her on this side of heaven again. I was distraught, angry, sad, and confused behind the death of my daughter. This sent me into such a very emotional state of depression. I began to experience mood swings. I would cry, I was very mean and irritated by others especially family members around me. I didn't want to talk or be around others, I would withdraw from everyone because I wanted to be alone. My thoughts at the time were, that my life was in turmoil because I was homeless, trying to start a new job, and at the same time, I was directionless about my relationship with the guy who had ask me to marry him. All this was a bit much, so I began to question God. I would say things like why is all of this happening in my life. Was it because I was living a sinful double life? I would blame myself for what happened to my daughter. However, the scripture says in **Isaiah 46:1 "God is our refuge and strength, a very present help in trouble."** At this point, I have to believe that no matter what happens in my life, God is with me, He knows what is best for me and He is always in control.

To help me get through this tough time, a very close friend of mine that we considered ourselves as family, paid for me an all expense trip to her lake house in Mississippi so that I could get away, heal, and sort things out. She arranged for me to enjoy Beale Street in Memphis dining at B.B. Kings Blues Club Restaurant. While I was there, I received a phone call reminding me that I was the speaker for a Women's Day Program; mind you, this engagement was the following week after my daughter's funeral. In my mind, I wasn't ready, or for that matter in any position to speak at their program. Upon speaking with the chairperson over that program, I wanted to tell her that I could not be the guest speaker. However, God would not allow me to cancel. God spoke to me quietly some empowering words; He said it's not about you it's about me.

> – *"So do not fear, for I am with you; do not be dismayed, for I am your God. I will strengthen you and help you. I will uphold you with my righteous right hand." Isaiah 41:10*

Nevertheless, I obeyed God and ended up being their guest speaker, God gave me a word, and it truly blessed them. I had women coming up to me sharing their testimonies. One woman testified and thanked me so much for giving that word; she said it helped her because she had lost her son in a car wreck traveling back to college. Another woman testified that she was on her way home and God told her to come to the program. She stated that I confirmed what God told her about transitioning to another job. It was a blessing to know, that after I shared my testimony of losing my daughter, being homeless, and at the same time receiving a job at a homeless shelter, and walking out on faith after quitting my job, that it help others. God was showing me that even though I was going through do not let it determine when, where, who, or how I help others.

- ***God is not unjust, he will not forget your work and the love you have shown him as you have helped his people and continue to help them***. ***Hebrews 6:10***

After all of that, I still at times found myself directionless and looking for things to do because my thoughts were all about Brittnay. Therefore, I could not gather myself to go back to work so, I quit my job as the director of the women and children shelter. However, I was so into myself because of what had happened to Brittnay I had no idea my son's were grieving as much as I was. They were so busy trying to keep me lifted up, that they did not get a chance to grieve so they could begin to move forward. It wasn't until later that I found out that they were actually going into a depression. They needed to talk about how they were feeling but had no one they could talk with. At that point, all they could do was give it to God. The bible tells us to **cast all your anxiety on Him because he cares for you. 1 Peter 5:7.**

CHAPTER 2

TURMOIL AND CONFUSION

Traumatized by losing Brittnay, I felt that I had chosen the wrong person. I was searching for and wanted to be loved. Therefore, I left the guy that I was living with and went back to the other guy that I was seeing. He's the one that I thought I should have married all along. In the process of much confusion and turmoil between the two men that I was in a relationship with, I made the choice to be with him and we decided to get married. After making this decision, my family and friends were in support of it. Therefore, we decided on a destination wedding ceremony in Jamaica that consisted of a total of eight.

Looking back, I knew when we were in Jamaica that I was not in love. I did all that because of the idea of being busy and having something to do in order to keep me from thinking about all that I had gone through. As funny, as this may sound, I realized all I desired was to go on a vacation. The reality of it was that we both were just each other's nurse mate. He was going through a lot and so was I. We were comforting each other and not truly getting to know one another. Two people attracted to a mere idol of whom we desired or wanted in each other. Simply put, we were trying to fill a void in our lives that only God could fill. With that being said, the wedding ceremony that we had in Jamaica was null and void because he was not officially divorced! Oh, wow! This was wrong and did not look good!

- ***Let marriage be held in honor among all, and let the marriage bed be undefiled, for God will judge the sexually immoral and adulterous. Hebrews 13:4***

- ***If we confess our sins, he is faithful and just to forgive us our sins and to cleanse us from all unrighteousness. 1John 1:9***

With giving reference to the word of God and reflecting back, the questions is, did I really want to stop being in this relationship? Did I, even think, acknowledge, or want to confess this as a sin; knowing what I knew about a man that I thought was divorced and now my "suppose to be new husband". As I said before, I did not love him; I was in love with what he could do for me and how he made me feel in my most vulnerable state of pain, turmoil, and confusion. Again, I was searching for happiness and a way to fill a void so that I could forget about Brittnay. Although this relationship was all wrong, at that time, the answer to the question asked earlier would have been NO.

We were in, the month October, and I was trying to see what I was going to do. However, because others were not able to come to Jamaica, we decided to have another wedding ceremony at a church in Shreveport so that our other family and friends could be a part and attend. Nevertheless, that meant I had to shop again for another wedding dress as well as bride maids dresses. In my mind, I thought I was doing the right thing because; again, I was searching for happiness, fulfillment and desiring to be whole no matter what I had to do to obtain it.

The night before the wedding my sisters and

friends rented a limo and we all went out to dinner in Natchitoches on the lake. Then we came back to Shreveport and went to different areas of town. We even stopped by different places in the city and lastly, we stopped at a nightclub. While all that was going on, I was hurting so bad down on the inside that I could not even enjoy all the planned activities and festivities that they were doing for me.

- *The LORD is close to the brokenhearted and saves those who are crushed in spirit. Psalms 34:18*

- *He sets on high those who are lowly, and those who mourn are lifted to safety. Job 5:11*

My second wedding day was finally here. The weather that day was very scary; we had such a bad thunderstorm. It was lighting, and thundering very hard. To my surprise, my wedding was very well attended; even with the weather being as bad as it was. However, the day of the wedding was true turmoil because one of my family members had been very upset because she was not in my wedding, she started so much confusion, and believe me, it was very noticeable. As we were preparing for the ceremony, I was already fearful because I just knew in my heart that she would show up and try to ruin everything. Sure enough, she showed up. I must say, in the midst of it all, my sisters coordinated my wedding and they did a fantastic and epic job in such short time. The church and wedding reception decorations was absolutely breath taking! It was fit for a queen and a king. Therefore, to me, any kind of confusion, distraction, or hindrances was not going to take away from or stop what my sisters did for me to make this day special. However, I knew in my heart that this second ceremony was not God ordained; after all, he was not officially divorced. I allowed my emotions to lead and guide me. With that being said, we should always rely on God in every area of our lives. This shows our faith and trust is in him and not in ourselves.

- *God will instruct me and teach me in the way I should go. He will guide me with His eye. Psalm 32:8*

After the wedding, my husband surprised me with a convertible two seater BMW. This was an early birthday present. Through my eyes and in my heart I needed to have things in order to be complete; so to me, and I was sure some others at the time would agree that this was the perfect gift! Nevertheless, even with that, I was still desiring and wanting more things. I loved to shop all the time and I still do but at that time, I would shop for things I solely desired and did not need. However, at that moment, I felt like a true Barbie doll. I was so happy after receiving the BMW but after while even that did not make me happy.

- *And he said to them, "Take care, and be on your guard against all covetousness, for one's life does not consist in the abundance of his possessions." Luke 12:15*

- *A good name is more desirable than great riches; to be esteemed is better than silver or gold. Proverbs 22:1*

Some time had passed; and he officially divorced. Nonetheless that did not matter to me because I was still grieving, looking for answers, and I continued to go in the wrong direction. I would hang out with friends, drink sociably, and eat at different restaurants that had live entertainment. I was trying to fit in where I definitely did not belong. I wanted the so-called in crowd (the world) to accept me. The bible says in **Romans 12:2 And be not conformed to this world: but be ye transformed by the renewing of your mind, that ye may prove what is that good, and acceptable, and perfect, will of God.** In other words, do not adopt the ways of the world or its wisdom. However, by this time, I was so confused with a messed up spiritual life, financial life, and personal life; it seemed like every area of my life was jacked up. My entire life was falling apart while I was trying to pretend everything was all right. The truth is, I really cared, but I just could not fix it.

- *"Come to me, all you who are weary and burdened, and I will give you rest. Take my yoke upon you and learn from me, for I am gentle and humble in heart, and you will find rest for your souls." Matthew 11:28-29*

In times like these, I can look back and know that God the Father was protecting me even when I was living foolishly. What father doesn't protect their child when their child does not know any better? God protects us when we try to do our own thing. God can see what we cannot see. If we are one of God's chosen children He is going to protect us whether we like it or not. What a Great! Great! Great! Father God is!

– *The LORD keeps you from all harm and watches over your life. The LORD keeps watch over you as you come and go, both now and forever. Psalm 121:7-8*

CHAPTER 3

DEALING WITH WHAT WAS BEFORE ME

Thanksgiving Holiday was approaching; it was the hardest time for me, after losing Brittnay. My birthday fell on Thanksgiving Day that year. However, I did not have the desire to be around anyone. I had mixed emotions, I wanted my family and friends to be more loving and have more sympathy for me, but instead it was nothing but turmoil and confusion because of some choices I made during my wedding ceremony. The same family member that I mention earlier is still offended because she was not in my wedding. Therefore, I was not communicating with some of my family members.

Thanksgiving and my birthday had finally arrived but I was praying that the day would be over real fast. I actually desired to sleep the entire day. I had dinner prepared and spent it with a select group of my choice of people. During that time, I announced to a few friends and family members that I thought about running for political office. Right after I made the announcement, they immediately told me I needed to join social media.

Once I joined, I learned how to post information and review other people's posts. I began to seek out my platform for running for political office. The pain was so intense, that I would try to keep myself busy so that I wouldn't think about losing Brittnay. Around that time, family and friends asked my husband and I about attending the Bayou Classic. I thought it would be a great getaway so we made the arrangements and we left early that Friday morning going to New Orleans. We spent time going shopping, going out to eat, and hanging out at local nightclubs. We had such a great time on our little getaway with our family and friends. I was really trying very hard to forget that Brittnay would not be in Shreveport when I returned.

After we returned home, I began to have mood swings and if any one asked me how I was, doing it would take all that I had to hold it together. For the life of me, I could not understand why some people would say the dumbest things to me. They would say, as time pass it will get better or you will be all right just keep busy. There was one particular incident that happen to me at the mall while I was shopping; I ran into an acquaintance, he was frowning up while looking at me, and said well it's good to see you, how have you been doing? Then the next thing he said to me was do not lose any more weight! I thought that was very insulting, so in return I said some things that made him feel very uncomfortable. I shared with him how I really viewed his appearance; and believe me; it was not nice at all. Listen; when a person is grieving please be careful of what you say to them, you do not know what their state of mind might be in at that moment in time. Others may not have noticed how I was grieving but to some it was evident how challenged I was after losing my daughter.

Leading up to the next major holiday was Christmas. I was so depressed that I did not want to do any shopping. I was not in the mood; my thoughts were, if I was not going to see Brittnay, what's the use of enjoying my life or the holidays for that matter. My emotions were all over the place; I didn't think about my sons or the fact that they were still here alive and that God allowed them to remain here with me on earth. I was not thinking that they wanted, and needed love from me as well. However, they never stop trying to offer me comfort, love on me, or do things with me. I tried to pretend that I enjoyed the different events they invited me to. However, nothing made me happy because all I could think about was Brittnay.

Furthermore, I wanted to do something different, I approached my New Year's traditional shopping that I would normally do in Shreveport with a new desire. As an alternative, I wanted to go to the mall in Monroe, LA to shop. I took this approach because I did not want to see the usual people; I just didn't want to be reminded of Brittnay and I did not want to have to talk to anybody. Therefore, my sister, a friend, and I went to the mall in Monroe and had a Blast.

While we were there, I thought about this reality show on television that captured my attention.

One of the cast members opened a restaurant and I desired to eat there, but it was not open that day so we posed for pictures in front of it. While we were there engaging in all the fun activities, I was still missing and thinking about Brittnay.

Upon my return home, I began setting the stage to do a public announcement about running for political office. I did a lot of research in order to get my team together for my fundraising events. I would utilize and joined other media outlets to build an audience. I began designing my flyers, postcards, campaign business cards, yard signs, t-shirts, buttons, and billboards. In my heart, I wanted this win so bad that I could taste it. This was my way of letting people know that I was not going to be defeated after losing my daughter. I wanted them to know I go hard.

My life motto is, **"Even the smallest person can change the twist of fate."** This motto reflects my attitude towards life and shows how you have hope when you deal with life's problems. I was born a fighter, that is why I never lose sight of my goals, and I will not give up before I reached them. I speak about my motto because it sums up some of my personal experiences, some of the choices, and some of the decisions that I make. Notice I said my motto because in the end and as a result I do understand that God's in control and knows what is best for me.

– *For I know the plans and thoughts that I have for you,' says the Lord, 'plans for peace and well-being and not for disaster to give you a future and a hope. Jeremiah 29:11*

CHAPTER 4

LIVING FOR MY PURPOSE SO I THOUGHT

Qualifying is fast approaching; for seven days a week, I would leave home early in the morning and return late at night. In the meantime my marriage was falling apart because I was never home and always on the go. Although, my sons were grown I was not spending time with them either. They were hurting inside but they were trying very hard not to show it. I have to admit my sons were trying to be strong. Nonetheless, I was having fundraisers attending political debates, and knocking on doors in the district that I was going to represent. I would speak to them about the importance and significance of voting as well as why they should vote for me. I spent numerous hours, days, weeks, and month trying to capture their attention. I was attending every event in my city; I was shaking hands, and stating why I was running for school board in district Two.

During my campaigning, I received the ultimate surprise; I was named Grand Marshal of the twenty-first, Annual Natchez Heritage Festival. This village was southeast of Natchitoches. It was the last home of the Natchez Indians, after the French defeated them in 1731. It was not until the Texas and the Pacific Railroad came through, that this village was established in 1938. Louisiana is the gateway to the Cane River National Heritage area. It is also the gateway for the Oakland Plantation, the Magnolia Complex, the Oak-lawn, and the Cherokee Plantation, (Private Homes).

My father was born and raised in Natchitoches, Louisiana on Cane River. It was truly an honor, to represent him. I had an opportunity to meet and greet with my family and many of my father's friends. It felt great to share in the love and joy exhibited during this special occasion. Through my pain, I celebrated and learned the history of my father's heritage from which I came.

Qualifying was finally here, so my team and I head to the courthouse to finish all my paperwork so that I could officially qualify. When I arrived everyone was cheering me on, and I loved every minute of it. I finished my paperwork and now it is official I was running for political office. I would get up early in the morning and stay up until late at night preparing nonstop seven days a week. However, I was not just doing political assignments to win the election; I was hanging out and in a relationship with an old friend; the same man that asked me to marry him the first time. The only reason, I married the other guy in the first place, is because in my mind I thought the first guy would not be able to take care of me; and truthfully, I didn't like the way he acted towards me, he would treat me as if he was envious of who I was. Nonetheless, there we were together again.

My old friend and I went to Vegas during the Mayweather fight, right in the middle of my campaign for his birthday. Yes, here I am married and in Vegas with the one, I really wanted to be with and marry no matter what I thought or how envious of me I felt he was. During that weekend in Vegas, I gambled and won a nice amount of money and I had an awesome time meeting and seeing so many people. With that being said, I was quickly trying to make up with my friend, and make him happy, so that he would forgive me for the choice I made by not choosing him. At one point on our trip, he attacked me and the craziest thing was that, I thought I deserved it because of the hurt I caused him. My thoughts were to win the election and divorce my husband so that he and I could be together.

It was not long before reality set in and he, because of how bad I had hurt him quickly reminded me by actually choking me, saying how bad I embarrassed and humiliated him in front of the whole entire world, especially his family and friends; He was mostly concerned with what they were saying about what I did to him. This was not the best or healthy situation or relationship for me. This was wrong.

I beseech you therefore, brethren, by the mercies of God, that ye present your bodies a living sacrifice, holy, acceptable unto God, [which is] your reasonable service. Romans12:1

When I returned home, things got busy for me. I was preparing to have more fundraisers. We were about two months away from the election; it was scheduled the first Saturday in November. I went all over district two going hard campaigning and meeting people. I would listen to them talk about improvements that they desired to see pertaining to the schools in the district. In the meantime, I went to church so that I could receive spiritual guidance. My emotions were all over the place; I was trying to avoid thinking about what happened back in Vegas knowing I was married, while at the same time, feeling like everyone was out to get me. You see, some of the choices that I made caused me not to trust anyone. All I can say is the attack of the enemy on the mind was real.

- *For the weapons of our warfare are not carnal, but mighty through God to the pulling down of strong holds ; Casting down imaginations, and every high thing that exalteth itself against the knowledge of God, and bringing into captivity every thought to the obedience of Christ; 2Corinthians10:4-5*

- *And after you have suffered a little while, the God of all grace, who has called you to His eternal glory in Christ, will Himself restore, confirm, strengthen, and establish you. 1Peter5:10*

In the midst of me running for political office, I felt like that was the worst time of my life. Therefore, I wanted everyone to feel sorry for me. News flash, they didn't and I could not seem to understand why. Nevertheless, I kept smiling as though I was happy inside. I was losing weight, not eating and still campaigning harder than ever. I was going to church on Wednesday, Sunday and every time we had an event at church. However, I only existed. In other words, I was attending church but not serving Christ with all my whole heart. I was still seeing and having relations with my ex, thinking we are going to have a future. He was leading me on. His only purpose was to hurt me because I hurt him. Knowing this, I kept going back and accepting the abuse. The abuse was not just physical but it was verbal and mental abuse.

– *The Lord is near to the brokenhearted and saves the crushed in spirit. Many are the afflictions of the righteous, but the Lord delivers him out of them all. He keeps all his bones; not one of them is broken. Psalm 34:18-20.*

Moving forward, I was out with my team at 3:00 am, the morning of the election, putting out yard signs all over the district. Mind you, this was a very large district! As soon as we were done, putting out the signs, my campaign team prayed and we all went out to breakfast. We all finished eating, assembled, and were ready to go because the polls opened up at 6:00 am. I drove through the district all morning, afternoon, and evening; meeting and greeting people, asking them to get out and vote, and reassuring them to vote for me; (Barbara Johnson Simpson) until the polls closed at 8:00 pm.

My campaign team booked the presidential suite at the Hilton Hotel. This is where we assembled at the end of the night for the election results. When the results came in, I was very nervous and could not keep still. In my mind, I was trying to win this for Brittnay in order to fill a void and mask the hurt because she was not there with me. I wanted to win this for those that hated on me and wished I wouldn't win at nothing. I wanted to win to show others that I was not defeated, I was not going to give up on myself, and to prove that I was a fighter that was not about to quit. At least that is what I told myself. The reality of all this was that deep down inside I wanted this victory for my haters. After all, I worked very hard day and night, meeting and greeting people, interviewing with news stations, and fundraising.

It's the end of the night; the results are in, which narrowed the race down to three candidates. The incumbent and I ended in a run-off. Therefore, I was angry with God, because my heart desired to win outright or lose all together. However, God saw differently, this meant that I had to campaign four more weeks. I was so confident that I would win; I went even harder than before knocking on doors in district two. I was so sure that I would win; that I even took a weekend off to attend the Bayou Classic in New Orleans knowingly the run-off election was only several days away.

While I was there spending time in New Orleans with my sister and friends, certain things took place that allowed God to show me that I'm not the only one in this world that go through tough situations in life. I believe God showed me this to remind me not to forget that we all have life experiences; the important thing is how we handle them, which determine our outcome. If we allow God to lead in every area of our lives (Spiritually, Personally, and financially) there are promises in His word that assures us that we have the victory. It's when we try to direct our own paths; things do not go as planned.

- ***Shew me thy ways, O LORD; teach me thy paths. Psalm 25:4***

I believe that God will allow us to experience things so that we can look back and know it was Him in control of our lives; However, He will also allow us to make our own decisions. That's the the beauty of God; He gives us free will.

We had four more weeks to campaign; Again, I would get up early in the morning and go to bed late at night. I did not consult with God; because I was upset with Him that I was in a run-off. I felt I could pull this off without God; all I needed was the people's ear. This was my first time running for political office and there I was in a run-off with the incumbent. I was pumped up in myself, as some would say I was arrogant. However, during that time I was only getting about 4 hours of sleep each night, I was having panic attacks because I feared losing. I desired with all my heart to win.

- ***Pride goeth before destruction and an haughty spirit before a fall. Proverbs 16:18***

I was up early Election Day. I was putting out signs and running non-stop until the polls closed. This would prove to be a great day! So I thought. We gathered at the Hilton Hotel again for the results of the election. I couldn't even watch the television, because I was in fear of losing. The results came in and it was devastating. Well, what do you know; I lost the race. Now, I am even more upset with God. He humiliated me and made me look like a loser. I was crying, embarrassed and nothing anyone said to me made sense. My Pastor was there with me; and she expounded on things, but what she shared did not register with me at that time.

- ***When a man's folly brings his way to ruin, his heart rages against the Lord. Proverbs 19:3***

Now, there I was dealing with facing the fact that I had lost the race. I felt so humiliated. I did not want to go out in public to face my haters. I felt and knew they were rejoicing over my loss.

Losing the election brought back the pain of me facing reality knowing that I will never physically see my daughter again on this earth. I was so depressed and humiliated to the point that the only time I would leave the house was when I went to church. I would go there with my appearance looking a mess. I did not have an appetite because of what was before me. That proved to me very unhealthy. Somehow, I kept moving forward, I kept pushing, and fighting to remain normal.

I was still trying to put up a great pretense that I had it all together, knowing I was living a double life and torn up inside. It's like the makeup we as women wear to cover-up a look that we are not confident with, wanting to take on another look that we feel is better than the look we already possess. **Proverbs 28:13 says, he who conceals his transgressions will not prosper, but he who confesses and forsakes them will find compassion.**

- *Nothing is covered up that will not be revealed, or hidden that will not be known. Luke12:2*

It has been a year now since Brittnay passed. Christmas holiday was approaching and I wanted everything imaginable. When I went shopping, I would purchase things that I really did not need. I was being selfish thinking of only a select few people that I had in mind to buy gifts. Often times we hear, it's better to give than to receive. I had a problem with that because it was a great thing for me to receive and to give to whom I desired. Basically, I would just reciprocate to the persons that would give to me.

On Christmas Day, I attended church service, I was feeling empty inside, while trying to rejoice. Afterwards I gathered with my family to exchange gifts. I didn't get what I expected and I was upset because to me it was no thought put into my gift. I decline the gift, and I knew it was wrong. However, now that I look back, I understand that the Lord loves and shows us that we should give from the heart cheerfully and not expecting to receive anything in return. When we give without expecting anything, in return we receive the blessings of the Lord.

New Year's was coming up and I was still

wondering in the wilderness. I tried to depend on others to get me out of my situation called life. I wavered over the fact I lost Brittnay. No matter what I knew, what the Lord showed me or what others said, I did not think anyone else situation was worse than mine. After all, I lost a child, a part of me. When I would see or talk to different people that were having difficulties, or that had lost a love one, it was, as if it didn't compare to my grief.

I was alone New Year's Eve watching television and grieving over my life. I felt in my heart I was at a point that I lost it all. I asked God why or how could I make so many of the same mistakes, repeating them over and over again. With that being said, I state this passage from the book of Exodus in my own words-when the Children of Israel were in the wilderness; Moses was leading them and they were not responding. God delivered them time after time and they were so ungrateful. He was continuously feeding them with food from heaven and blessing them but they continued to want more without committing themselves to God whole-heartedly. My life at that time reminded me of when the Children of

Israel were in the wilderness. Just Like them, God gave me so many opportunities to come unto him; but I desired to do it my way. God knows what he has placed inside us; often times we do not understand until we have true repentance; then that which is inside of us will begin to manifest.

– *No man can come to me, except the Father which hath sent me draw him: and I will raise him up at the last day. It is written in the prophets, and they shall be all taught of God. Every man therefore, that hath heard, and hath learned of the Father, cometh unto me. John 6:44-45*

We were officially in the New Year and I had not begun to grasp that I was still wondering in the wilderness. In the meantime, the other man and I are still seeing each other intimately and going places together. My husband asked me what my plans were, and I in return said, "You signed up for this marriage you figure it out" because your job as my husband is to provide for me a lavish lifestyle. What I basically meant was; he couldn't take care of me, I married the wrong man.

— *And he said unto them, Take heed, and beware of covetousness: for a man's life consisteth not in the abundance of the things which he possesseth. Luke 12:15*

There I was looking for a job, trying to get over the fact that my daughter had passed, my marriage was in trouble, I didn't win the election, and it seemed like everyone I turned to that I thought would be there to help me pick up the pieces of my life had turned their back on me. I thought to myself, when I was campaigning and things were looking good the momentum was in my favor, everybody had my back. You see, everyone loves a winner; but people will abandon ship if they see that you are not the victor.

— *Many are the afflictions of the righteous: but the LORD delivereth him out of them all. Psalm 34:19*

CHAPTER 5

I SHALL NOT DIE! BUT LIVE!

— *__Submit yourselves therefore to God. Resist the devil, and he will flee from you.__*
__James 4:7__

I had began having thoughts of suicide. I would hear voices in my head telling me to jump off the 220 bridge. I did not know which way to turn. Therefore, I called my Pastor and I asked if we could meet at the church so that we could have a prayer intervention. After praying and talking with the pastor, I was still not doing well. I was faking as though I was doing great. However, those same thoughts remained so I made up my mind to put it in to action.

I was on my way to church one Sunday and I decided I was going to Natchitoches, Louisiana to visit my family, purchase some pills, and commit suicide. Well, that is just what I did.

After returning from Natchitoches I went to my son's apartment, I took the pills that I had purchased, and I layed in his bed to die. I was very drowsy; I was going in and out of sleep and every time I would wake up, I kept saying, God hear my cry; I am ready to die; I do not want to live anymore; I have nothing to live for.

After so long, time passed, nothing happened, so I took more pills and then I felt myself going unconscious. Somehow, I made it to my son's bathroom; at this point, I was actually scared that I was going to die for real. Immediately, I cried out to God saying please God do not take me! I will do whatever you want me to do. I will do whatever you tell me to do. Then I fell to the floor and it was as if I was in another zone and a mighty wind came in and gave me breath. I got up, I vomited, and I kept vomiting repeatedly. I was so tired, sleepy, and drained but I was afraid to close my eyes and go to sleep because I thought I was not going wake up.

- *I shall not die, but live, and declare the works of the LORD. Psalm 118:17*

The next morning I went back to my house scared and confused. I called my doctor's office, made an appointment so that I could check on my health; I lost so much weight from not eating. I must say, my doctor's visit was very therapeutic. It actually turned into a coaching and counseling session. I was able to talk about what I was going through at different times after my daughter passed away. My doctor prescribed for me some sleeping pills as well as some medicine normally prescribed to children to give them an appetite. I did not take but one sleeping pill because I realized that it made me more alert and awake instead of sleep.

I finally have an appetite again; I had much energy, I felt so much better, and I wanted to exercise. I began to search for employment. I was going to church and actively involved at Bible Study, Sunday school and other church services. However, I was going through the motion while in church. I was married acting as those I was single. I would go to different events alone to show or act as if I was not married. People would ask me about my relationship and I would say I am not happy, I married for the wrong reason, he is a good guy, but he is not for me. I went on as though I was available and acting as if it was okay to see other people; and it didn't bother me.

- *If anyone, then, knows the good they ought to do and doesn't do it, it is sin for them.*
  James 4:17

- *You have heard that it was said, 'You shall not commit adultery. 'But I tell you that anyone who looks at a woman lustfully has already committed adultery with her in his heart. Matthew 5:27-28*

It has been a while since Brittnay passed, and I was at a point where I had to face the fact that my Brittnay is gone. God was drawing me close to Him and I did not understand what I was doing or where I suppose to be in my relationship with God. Furthermore, I was still angry about losing the election. One day God spoke to me and said these words: you know how hard you ran your campaign for the political office that you were pursuing? That is how hard you will run to build up my Kingdom. Your heart desired to serve as school board representative for district two. You, being, a servant in the Kingdom is far greater than any office. With that being said the bible states, in John **6:63 it is the spirit that quickeneth; the flesh profiteth nothing; the words that I speak unto you, they are spirit, and they are life.** Let me tell you, what God said to me was not what I had planned for my life. I wanted to serve in a capacity that I felt I had people's attention, such as working with and making decisions for our youth. I could not understand the logic behind God putting such a mandate on my life at that time. However, the scripture says **for he is our God; and we are the people of his pasture, and the sheep of his hand. Today if ye will hear his voice, Harden not your heart, as in the provocation, and as in the day of temptation in the wilderness: Psalms 95:7-8.**

– *For many are called, but few are chosen. Matthew 22:14*

CHAPTER 6

GOD REVEALED TO ME WHO I WAS IN HIM

With so much going on in my life, I was looking to have a good time. Therefore, timing was perfect for my good friend to invite me to a class reunion party. I accepted the invitation to attend and I brought along a mutual girlfriend. While I was there, a young man originally from Louisiana but no longer lived there introduce himself to me. We laughed talked and exchanged numbers. As we continue to communicate, I told him my status that I was unhappily married and that I would be filing for divorce very soon.

As time went on, my new friend asked me if I wanted to go on a date with him and I accepted. I decided, because I desired to go to Puerto Rico for my birthday and thanksgiving that this would be a perfect place to go for our first date. We spent several days there, however, I was having fun one minute, and then the next minute I was back in the reality that Brittnay was gone. My mood would change from happy too sad. My thoughts were always on Brittnay. Never once thinking I was married and had a husband.

Once we returned from our trip, every time we had a conversation it seemed like we would talk non-stop. Overtime, we decided to go on another date. He liked the Dallas Cowboys and so did I. We flew to Dallas, spent time talking over dinner, did some shopping, and of course, we enjoyed the Dallas Cowboys game. In the midst of all this, I had to face the fact that I did not want to be married anymore. There I was, trying to figure out how I was going to end this marriage. Without question, I was definitely not going to stay in any situation that I was not happy in.

I finally arranged to talk with my husband. Unlike me, he wanted to talk so that we could work together to save our marriage. I knew going into the conversation that I had to come clean with him because he already knew I had been involved with my ex. He knew, because, people in our city told him information about me. Nevertheless, I felt bad and did not want to hurt him so I did not share my true feelings about me seeing my ex, nor that I was dating a new guy or me wanting a divorce. I went on allowing him to believe that all was well and that we could continue as though we were going to make our marriage work. During our conversation, he shared with me that some people wanted our marriage to fail. After he said those words to me, divorce was no longer our conversation or an option because in my mind I did not want to be a failure so I continued to pretend I was happily married.

As time went on, I still acted as though I was single and kept on dating. Then I realized I liked being able to do what my heart desired whenever I desired. I talked to my soon to be ex-husband and I explained to him that I was not happy and that I was truly sorry but I could not go on like this; so I asked for a divorce. He tried several times to talk me out of it. However, the one thing that was certain in my heart was that I was not in love with him, and I could not fake it any longer.

I reached out to my attorney in order to file for divorce. Soon after, I spoke to my husband and shared with him that this would be a simple process: just show up, agree, and sign the divorce papers. I told him if he did that, the court would not have to serve him a petition to answer. Did he show up for the court date? NO.

Later on, my attorney spoke with him on the phone while we were outside the courtroom. My husband stated that he would go ahead and show up the following week to sign divorce papers before the judge. He finally signed the papers. My divorce was final.

Here it is, one day, I find myself speaking to my ex-husband crying and upset. He was very hurt behind our divorce so he asked me if he could go and talk with one of my sons about what happened. I broke down and cried so hard, I told him that I didn't mean to hurt him the way that I did. I felt so bad and I was hurting inside. A couple days later, he called and texted me inviting me over to his house, and he volunteered to come by to pick me up. Nonetheless, I did not go with him because I was afraid of hurting the man that I was dating.

Moving ahead, I was flying in and out of town with the man that I had been dating. While being with him, I got a job as a MPH counselor for a company. I was working, attending church, and doing other activities with my Sorority. One day my spiritual leader told me about spending time with my sons. My thoughts were, why, is my leader telling me to spend time with my children. Deep down inside, I knew it was because in the beginning when Brittnay had passed away I didn't spend enough time with them. Nevertheless, I obeyed, and as time passed; I started talking to them on a regular basis and I spent more quality time with them. We would go to dinner, shopping and just having a great time with each other on a regular basis.

In the beginning, I failed to mention, that right before my divorce, I was having problems with nosebleeds and blood clots coming out of my mouth. This irregular bleeding was happening off and on. I became very scared and nervous so I made a doctor's appointment to have it checked out; but I did not get a chance to go because I couldn't afford to pay the co-pay. As time went, the bleeding stopped for good, so I was no longer worried, but I often wondered why the irregular bleeding started in the first place.

After experiencing that, I began having panic attacks. I felt as though I was going to die so I would be scared to go to sleep at night. At first, it would happen every so often then it started more frequently. I didn't know what to do. One time, while I was in church, I prayed and asked the Lord why was I so scared and why was I so afraid that I was going to die. No matter how much I prayed or what answer the Lord said to me, I would still be very fearful about what was going on in my life.

– *For God has not given us a spirit of fear, but of power and of love and of a sound mind. 2 Timothy 1:7*

By this time, I felt things were too bad for me, so in my heart I wanted to get away. I didn't want to live in Shreveport anymore because I lost my daughter, I was faced with the embarrassment of losing material things, (car, house, and land), I lost the election, I felt I married the wrong person, I divorced, which made three marriages that had failed, I couldn't find the right job and I had made other bad choices. There was so much going on with me over the course of time that I thought I lost my status in the world; but, yet and still, I knew that this was a wilderness experience for me. However, in the midst of all that God my father revealed to me **Romans 12: 2, which says, and be not conformed to this world: but be ye transformed by the renewing of your mind, that ye may prove what is that good, and acceptable, and perfect, will of God.**

By this time, I was going through real bad and I ignored the revelation of what God was revealing personally to me in Romans 12:2. However, it is clear to me now that the great enemy of this renewal is, conforming to this world. We have to watch for engaging in plans for happiness, as though our happiness comes from the things of this world, which is only temporal and will soon pass away. We should do our best not to fall in with the traditions of those who walk in the lusts of the flesh, and mind earthly things. To do this or even overcome this, we must allow the work of the Holy Spirit to lead, guide, and teach us. When we allow that to happen, the spirit will begin to work in our understanding, and is carried over to our will, affections, and conversation until there is a change of our whole man into the image and likeness of God. Furthermore, we have to give ourselves whole heartily to God in order not to conform to this world and with the help of the Holy spirit walk in the knowledge of God, The righteousness of God, and true holiness of God.

Despite of what I was feeling, I went out of town visiting and I was there longer than I expected. While I was there, I needed to get my hair done so I went online and Google beauty shops and I found one; I called, and made an appointment. Once I got to the beauty shop to get my hair done, my beautician notice that I am Greek, she tells me that she has other Greek clients whose hair she does and they are my sisters. She told me, she would give them my number so that they could call me. Eventually my sisters called me and the following week I went to a meeting. After that, they invited me to a sorority event which was held during the church service. After attending that Sunday, I decided to go back again the next Sunday and I also went to bible study the following Wednesday.

After attending church service there for a while, one day a friend and I decided to go out to dinner. While we were eating I had another panic attack, and again I thought I was going to die. I was very scared so I spoke with a friend of mine who is a minister and I shared with him what happened to me on several different occasions and he told me that certain things were happening with me especially the fear and panic attacks because God was trying to get my attention. I'm reminded of the scripture that says, **Fear not, for I am with you; be not dismayed, for I am your God; I will strengthen you, I will help you, I will uphold you with my righteous right hand. Isaiah 41:10**

After the minister shared with me that God was trying to get my attention, I did not waste any time, I went on a fast because I wanted to hear from God clearly. After doing a fast, God released to me that he does not dwell in an unclean temple. I immediately shared with my friend the one that I was dating, what God released to me. I asked God how He is going to handle that. God's response to me was I am your father and you will keep my word.

- *If ye love me, keep my commandments. John 14:15*

When God is leading and guiding He has already taken care of his desired outcome.

- *But now thus says the LORD, he who created you, O Jacob, he who formed you, O Israel: "Fear not, for I have redeemed you; I have called you by name, you are mine. When you pass through the waters, I will be with you; and through the rivers, they shall not overwhelm you; when you walk through fire you shall not be burned, and the flame shall not consume you. Isaiah 43:1-2*

Looking back, I committed adultery in the past and now I was committing fornication and living with a man, shacking is what we call it. The bible tells us to **flee fornication. Every sin that a man does is without the body; but he that commits fornication sins against his own body. 1 Corinthians 6:18.** I had to make a choice and I soon did.

When I separated from sin, I wanted to know God on a more personal level. God began to work in my life and drawing me closer to him by reading His word, praying to him, and asking him what he would have me to do in order to be completely healed and delivered.

God shared with me that I had to repent of all my sins and make a confession. I repented and I confessed and believe that Jesus Christ died on the cross and rose from the dead for my sins so that I would have the right to eternal life. **Romans 10:9-10 says, that if thou shalt confess with thy mouth the Lord Jesus, and shalt believe in thine heart that God hath raised him from the dead, thou shalt be saved. For with the heart man believeth unto righteousness; and with the mouth confession is made unto salvation.**

God revealed to me true repentance is what he desires from me. Once I truly repented, God began to direct me to apologize to certain people that I had wronged. He also gave me peace with those that would not accept my apologies and me repenting from my faults. I began to have a strong desire to give and sow seeds. I even had a desire to bless others and when I did, I gave all the credit and the glory to God for placing it in my heart. I must say, that I had so much joy and confidence with the new me when I got saved, that I desired for family members, friends, strangers, and everyone around me to be saved.

> *— You make known to me the path of life; in your presence there is fullness of joy; at your right hand are pleasures forevermore. Psalm 16:11*

With my new life in Christ, I have come to realize that transformation starts as soon as we truly repent. Starting from scratch is how God rebuilds us. The bible teaches us in **2 Corinthians 5:17 therefore, if anyone is in Christ, he is a new creation. The old has passed away; behold, the new has come.**

> *— No temptation has overtaken you that is not common to man. God is faithful, and he will not let you be tempted beyond your ability, but with the temptation he will also provide the way of escape, that you may be able to endure it. 1Corinthians 10:13*

PRAISE BREAK
I Just Want To Say Thank You!

I thank you Father for saving me! I thank you for your mercy and your grace! You were always there, your love over shadowed me in what I thought was my darkest hour. You were right there in the middle, and your hands were always there to protect me. It was you Father, who allowed me to overcome a life of turmoil and confusion.

I thank you Father for the fight I had in me back then and in me now, this gives me the drive to come out on the winning side. I am no longer the victim but I am the victor! I am more than a conquer!

Thank you Father for revealing to me who I am in you!

AS I LOOK BACK AND THINK THINGS OVER

God reminded me when I was pregnant, I asked for a girl. I had so much faith that he would give me the desire of my heart. I chose her name Brittnay Nashay. I imagined, while I was carrying her in my stomach that I would love her so much, she would be so beautiful, loving, and kind. God already knew that my heart loved her. When Brit Brit was 9 years old, she was diagnosed with juvenile diabetes and the only option she had was to take insulin shots, in which she was suppose to take three times a day. She did not like being a diabetic; she would sneak and not take her medicine and eat all the wrong foods.

I would like to add, Type 1 diabetes or Juvenile diabetes is serious. There is no cure, and it requires constant careful self-management (proper rest, a healthy diet, exercise, and good medical care). We are to be good stewards over our bodies in everything and at all times. **The bible says in 1Corinthians 6:19 Do you not know that your bodies are temples of the Holy Spirit, who is in you, whom you have received from God? You are not your own;**

The day Brittnay passed we had a three-way conversation with my mother. I recall hearing her voice so vivid today. Britt Britt kept repeating you called momma on me. However, little did I know God was calling Brittnay home. I believe God was making a three-way call when he visited me while I was sitting at the duck pond. His voice whispered pray for Brittnay. I immediately prayed let your will be done in her life. I did not pray for healing; my faith was in God's will for her life. I did not know that she would pass away a couple hours later.

As I look back now, I understand that God was showing me **Death and life *are* in the power of the tongue: and they that love it shall eat the fruit thereof. Proverbs 18:21**. As I said earlier and I will say it again if I knew then what I know

now I would not have prayed that prayer. But I found out in going through that it's not about me and what I want, or how I feel it's all about My Lord and Savior Jesus Christ! In the end, God gets all of the praise, honor, and the glory!

THE CONFESSION

Brittnay is truly missed and she will be forever loved in my heart. The one thing that gives me great joy is that she confessed Romans 10:9 and she believed Jesus died on the cross for her sins, and rose from the dead so that we have the right to eternal life, and because of her confession, I have peace she rests with our Heavenly Father.

It is a blessing now to look back on all the things that happened on our beautiful journey together.

Amen!

A CHRISTIAN BEDTIME PRAYER

Now I lay me down to sleep,
I pray the Lord my soul to keep;
If I should die before I wake,
I pray to the Lord my soul to take.
Amen

Rest In Heaven (RIH)

My Sweet Princess "Britt Britt"

CONCLUSION

After, ceaseless running to no avail; God called me into the ministry with exultation. I accepted God's call on my life. I have come to know that in every situation God is our only true source. **God is our refuge and strength, a present help in trouble. Psalm 46:1**

- *Do not remember the former things,*
  Or ponder the things of the past. Isaiah 43:18

Currently I am (MIT) Minister In Training; under the leadership of Bishop Larry Brandon and Co Pastor Wanda Brandon. Upon completion of my ministerial training, I will pursue writing a second book.

 I give thanks to my Heavenly Father, which placed everything on the inside of me to write a book that pertains to a portion of my life. Thank you Prophetess Corliss Meredith, for allowing God to use you for the provision on how to put together a small portion of my life testimony and illustrate it in a form of a book so others can read and share in my experiences.

FINAL THOUGHTS

I believe God will allow us to go through situations and circumstances so that we end up where he wants us to be even if we don't have any conscious part in getting there.

When life doesn't seem fair seek God first with your whole heart. Second, turn to Him in prayer. Next, lift up the situation and those involved to him. Then, in your own way, while, humbly praying, ask Him for the things **listed below**. Last, allow His love to over shadow you.

- ✓ **Strength:** asking this will strengthen you in your weakness to allow you to keep going.

- ✓ **Peace:** asking this will give you peace when you are hurting and broken.

- ✓ **Directions:** asking this will help direct you specifically about what to do and what not to do.

- ✓ **Discernment:** asking this will help you follow God's leading through the process of spiritual application of biblical truth that fit your situation.

- ✓ **Protection:** asking this will allow the Lord to protect you when you feel defenseless.

God Bless You!

Notes

References:

King James Bible

New King James Bible Version (NKJV)

Amplified Bible Version (AMP)

American Standard Version (ASV)

New International Version (NIV)

English Standard Version (ESV)

Children Bedtime Prayer
The New England Primer, 1750 ed., p. 28
http://cdlrsandbox.org/neprimer/versiontwopages/028.html

New England Primer: A Primary Source Website is licensed under a Creative Commons Attribution-NonCommercial-ShareAlike 3.0 Unported License. Last updated: 11/20/2013

Print Layout/Interior/Editing-by: Corliss Y. Meredith
With Ready Writer Publishing

Book cover created, and illustrated by:
Melissa Casole
http://www.thirdidsignz.com

Stay connected with

Barbara Johnson-Simpson

By logging on to her website

www.barbarasimpsonbook.com

You can also email her@

shrevbarbara1908@yahoo.com

or connect with her on

Social Media

Face book:

Barbara Johnson-Simpson

Instagram:

Barbie1908

Twitter:

@Barbieboo1908

Periscope:

Barbara Simpson@Barbie1908

About The Author

Barbara Johnson Simpson is the mother of three. Born and raised in Shreveport, Louisiana graduating Fair Park High School. She furthered her education, graduating from Southern University in Shreveport, Louisiana. She also attended Wiley College in Marshall, Texas and received her Master's Degree at Grambling State University.

Barbara enjoyed a career spanning from working in municipal entities parish and city government, a K-12 educator, and a Director of a homeless shelter for women and children. Barbara has experience in the financial banking. She has also worked as a mental health professional.

Barbara successfully, ran a political campaign for Caddo Parish School Board District Two run-off election, while serving on the Northwest Louisiana Human Service District Board and second Vice President of the NAACP Shreveport Chapter. She continues to serve Alpha Kappa Alpha Sorority, Incorporated.

Barbara lives and is available in two locations: The greater Chicago area, and Shreveport Louisiana, where she is a minister in training, up under the leadership of Bishop, Larry Lawrence Brandon, of Praise Temple Full Gospel Shreveport.

Overcoming A Life of Turmoil

www.ingramcontent.com/pod-product-compliance
Lightning Source LLC
Chambersburg PA
CBHW070134100426
42744CB00009B/1829